£10.95

O'Flaherty V.C.

George Bernard Shaw

O'Flaherty V.C.

Table of Contents

O'Flaherty V.C.

George Bernard Shaw

Kessinger Publishing reprints thousands of hard–to–find books!

O'Flaherty V.C.

O'FLAHERTY V.C.: A RECRUITING PAMPHLET

O'Flaherty V.C.

It may surprise some people to learn that in 1915 this little play was a recruiting poster in disguise. The British officer seldom likes Irish soldiers; but he always tries to have a certain proportion of them in his battalion, because, partly from a want of common sense which leads them to value their lives less than Englishmen do (lives are really less worth living in a poor country), and partly because even the most cowardly Irishman feels obliged to outdo an Englishman in bravery if possible, and at least to set a perilous pace for him, Irish soldiers give impetus to those military operations which require for their spirited execution more devilment than prudence.

Unfortunately, Irish recruiting was badly bungled in 1915. The Irish were for the most part Roman Catholics and loyal Irishmen, which means that from the English point of view they were heretics and rebels. But they were willing enough to go soldiering on the side of France and see the world outside Ireland, which is a dull place to live in. It was quite easy to enlist them by approaching them from their own point of view. But the War Office insisted on approaching them from the point of view of Dublin Castle. They were discouraged and repulsed by refusals to give commissions to Roman Catholic officers, or to allow distinct Irish units to be formed. To attract them, the walls were covered with placards headed REMEMBER BELGIUM. The folly of asking an Irishman to remember anything when you want him to fight for England was apparent to everyone outside the Castle: FORGET AND FORGIVE would have been more to the point. Remembering Belgium and its broken treaty led Irishmen to remember Limerick and its broken treaty; and the recruiting ended in a rebellion, in suppressing which the British artillery quite unnecessarily reduced the centre of Dublin to ruins, and the British commanders killed their leading prisoners of war in cold blood morning after morning with an effect of long–drawn–out ferocity. Really it was only the usual childish petulance in which John Bull does things in a week that disgrace him for a century, though he soon recovers his good humor, and cannot understand why the survivors of his wrath do not feel as jolly with him as he does with them. On the smouldering ruins of Dublin the appeals to remember Louvain were presently supplemented by a fresh appeal. IRISHMEN, DO YOU WISH TO HAVE THE HORRORS OF WAR BROUGHT TO YOUR OWN HEARTHS AND HOMES? Dublin laughed sourly.

As for me I addressed myself quite simply to the business of obtaining recruits. I knew by personal experience and observation what anyone might have inferred from the records of Irish emigration, that all an Irishman's hopes and ambitions turn on his opportunities of getting out of Ireland. Stimulate his loyalty, and he will stay in Ireland and die for her;

for, incomprehensible as it seems to an Englishman, Irish patriotism does not take the form of devotion to England and England's king. Appeal to his discontent, his deadly boredom, his thwarted curiosity and desire for change and adventure, and, to escape from Ireland, he will go abroad to risk his life for France, for the Papal States, for secession in America, and even, if no better may be, for England. Knowing that the ignorance and insularity of the Irishman is a danger to himself and to his neighbors, I had no scruple in making that appeal when there was something for him to fight which the whole world had to fight unless it meant to come under the jack boot of the German version of Dublin Castle.

There was another consideration, unmentionable by the recruiting sergeants and war orators, which must nevertheless have helped them powerfully in procuring soldiers by voluntary enlistment. The happy home of the idealist may become common under millennial conditions. It is not common at present. No one will ever know how many men joined the army in 1914 and 1915 to escape from tyrants and taskmasters, termagants and shrews, none of whom are any the less irksome when they happen by ill–luck to be also our fathers, our mothers, our wives and our children. Even at their amiablest, a holiday from them may be a tempting change for all parties. That is why I did not endow O'Flaherty V.C. with an ideal Irish colleen for his sweetheart, and gave him for his mother a Volumnia of the potato patch rather than a affectionate parent from whom he could not so easily have torn himself away.

I need hardly say that a play thus carefully adapted to its purpose was voted utterly inadmissible; and in due course the British Government, frightened out of its wits for the moment by the rout of the Fifth Army, ordained Irish Conscription, and then did not dare to go through with it. I still think my own line was the more businesslike. But during the war everyone except the soldiers at the front imagined that nothing but an extreme assertion of our most passionate prejudices, without the smallest regard to their effect on others, could win the war. Finally the British blockade won the war; but the wonder is that the British blockhead did not lose it. I suppose the enemy was no wiser. War is not a sharpener of wits; and I am afraid I gave great offence by keeping my head in this matter of Irish recruiting. What can I do but apologize, and publish the play now that it can no longer do any good?

O'FLAHERTY V.C.

At the door of an Irish country house in a park. Fine, summer weather; the summer of 1916. The porch, painted white, projects into the drive: but the door is at the side and the front has a window. The porch faces east: and the door is in the north side of it. On the south side is a tree in which a thrush is singing. Under the window is a garden seat with an iron chair at each end of it.

The last four bars of God Save the King are heard in the distance, followed by three cheers. Then the band strikes up It's a Long Way to Tipperary and recedes until it is out of hearing.

Private O'Flaherty V.C. comes wearily southward along the drive, and falls exhausted into the garden seat. The thrush utters a note of alarm and flies away. The tramp of a horse is heard.

A GENTLEMAN'S VOICE. Tim! Hi! Tim! [He is heard dismounting.]

A LABORER'S VOICE. Yes, your honor.

THE GENTLEMAN'S VOICE. Take this horse to the stables, will you?

A LABORER'S VOICE. Right, your honor. Yup there. Gwan now. Gwan. [The horse is led away.]

General Sir Pearce Madigan, an elderly baronet in khaki, beaming with enthusiasm, arrives. O'Flaherty rises and stands at attention.

SIR PEARCE. No, no, O'Flaherty: none of that now. You're off duty. Remember that though I am a general of forty years service, that little Cross of yours gives you a higher rank in the roll of glory than I can pretend to.

O'FLAHERTY [relaxing]. I'm thankful to you, Sir Pearce; but I wouldn't have anyone think that the baronet of my native place would let a common soldier like me sit down in his presence without leave.

SIR PEARCE. Well, you're not a common soldier, O'Flaherty: you're a very uncommon one; and I'm proud to have you for my guest here today.

5

O'Flaherty V.C.

O'FLAHERTY. Sure I know, sir. You have to put up with a lot from the like of me for the sake of the recruiting. All the quality shakes hands with me and says they're proud to know me, just the way the king said when he pinned the Cross on me. And it's as true as I'm standing here, sir, the queen said to me: "I hear you were born on the estate of General Madigan," she says; "and the General himself tells me you were always a fine young fellow." "Bedad, Mam," I says to her, "if the General knew all the rabbits I snared on him, and all the salmon I snatched on him, and all the cows I milked on him, he'd think me the finest ornament for the county jail he ever sent there for poaching."

SIR PEARCE [Laughing]. You're welcome to them all, my lad. Come [he makes him sit down again on the garden seat]! sit down and enjoy your holiday [he sits down on one of the iron chairs; the one at the doorless side of the porch.]

O'FLAHERTY. Holiday, is it? I'd give five shillings to be back in the trenches for the sake of a little rest and quiet. I never knew what hard work was till I took to recruiting. What with the standing on my legs all day, and the shaking hands, and the making speeches, and—what's worse—the listening to them and the calling for cheers for king and country, and the saluting the flag till I'm stiff with it, and the listening to them playing God Save the King and Tipperary, and the trying to make my eyes look moist like a man in a picture book, I'm that bet that I hardly get a wink of sleep. I give you my word, Sir Pearce, that I never heard the tune of Tipperary in my life till I came back from Flanders; and already it's drove me to that pitch of tiredness of it that when a poor little innocent slip of a boy in the street the other night drew himself up and saluted and began whistling it at me, I clouted his head for him, God forgive me.

SIR PEARCE [soothingly]. Yes, yes: I know. I know. One does get fed up with it: I've been dog tired myself on parade many a time. But still, you know, there's a gratifying side to it, too. After all, he is our king; and it's our own country, isn't it?

O'FLAHERTY. Well, sir, to you that have an estate in it, it would feel like your country. But the divil a perch of it ever I owned. And as to the king: God help him, my mother would have taken the skin off my back if I'd ever let on to have any other king than Parnell.

SIR PEARCE [rising, painfully shocked]. Your mother! What are you dreaming about, O'Flaherty? A most loyal woman. Always most loyal. Whenever there is an illness in the

Royal Family, she asks me every time we meet about the health of the patient as anxiously as if it were yourself, her only son.

O'FLAHERTY. Well, she's my mother; and I won't utter a word agen her. But I'm not saying a word of lie when I tell you that that old woman is the biggest kanatt from here to the cross of Monasterboice. Sure she's the wildest Fenian and rebel, and always has been, that ever taught a poor innocent lad like myself to pray night and morning to St Patrick to clear the English out of Ireland the same as he cleared the snakes. You'll be surprised at my telling you that now, maybe, Sir Pearce?

SIR PEARCE [unable to keep still, walking away from O'Flaherty]. Surprised! I'm more than surprised, O'Flaherty. I'm overwhelmed. [Turning and facing him.] Are you—are you joking?

O'FLAHERTY. If you'd been brought up by my mother, sir, you'd know better than to joke about her. What I'm telling you is the truth; and I wouldn't tell it to you if I could see my way to get out of the fix I'll be in when my mother comes here this day to see her boy in his glory, and she after thinking all the time it was against the English I was fighting.

SIR PEARCE. Do you mean to say you told her such a monstrous falsehood as that you were fighting in the German army?

O'FLAHERTY. I never told her one word that wasn't the truth and nothing but the truth. I told her I was going to fight for the French and for the Russians; and sure who ever heard of the French or the Russians doing anything to the English but fighting them? That was how it was, sir. And sure the poor woman kissed me and went about the house singing in her old cracky voice that the French was on the sea, and they'd be here without delay, and the Orange will decay, says the Shan Van Vocht.

SIR PEARCE [sitting down again, exhausted by his feelings]. Well, I never could have believed this. Never. What do you suppose will happen when she finds out?

O'FLAHERTY. She mustn't find out. It's not that she'd half kill me, as big as I am and as brave as I am. It's that I'm fond of her, and can't bring myself to break the heart in her. You may think it queer that a man should be fond of his mother, sir, and she having bet him from the time he could feel to the time she was too slow to ketch him; but I'm fond

7

of her; and I'm not ashamed of it. Besides, didn't she win the Cross for me?

SIR PEARCE. Your mother! How?

O'FLAHERTY. By bringing me up to be more afraid of running away than of fighting. I was timid by nature; and when the other boys hurted me, I'd want to run away and cry. But she whaled me for disgracing the blood of the O'Flahertys until I'd have fought the divil himself sooner than face her after funking a fight. That was how I got to know that fighting was easier than it looked, and that the others was as much afeard of me as I was of them, and that if I only held out long enough they'd lose heart and give rip. That's the way I came to be so courageous. I tell you, Sir Pearce, if the German army had been brought up by my mother, the Kaiser would be dining in the banqueting hall at Buckingham Palace this day, and King George polishing his jack boots for him in the scullery.

SIR PEARCE. But I don't like this, O'Flaherty. You can't go on deceiving your mother, you know. It's not right.

O'FLAHERTY. Can't go on deceiving her, can't I? It's little you know what a son's love can do, sir. Did you ever notice what a ready liar I am?

SIR PEARCE. Well, in recruiting a man gets carried away. I stretch it a bit occasionally myself. After all, it's for king and country. But if you won't mind my saying it, O'Flaherty, I think that story about your fighting the Kaiser and the twelve giants of the Prussian guard singlehanded would be the better for a little toning down. I don't ask you to drop it, you know; for it's popular, undoubtedly; but still, the truth is the truth. Don't you think it would fetch in almost as many recruits if you reduced the number of guardsmen to six?

O'FLAHERTY. You're not used to telling lies like I am, sir. I got great practice at home with my mother. What with saving my skin when I was young and thoughtless, and sparing her feelings when I was old enough to understand them, I've hardly told my mother the truth twice a year since I was born; and would you have me turn round on her and tell it now, when she's looking to have some peace and quiet in her old age?

SIR PEARCE (troubled in his conscience]. Well, it's not my affair, of course, O'Flaherty. But hadn't you better talk to Father Quinlan about it?

O'FLAHERTY. Talk to Father Quinlan, is it! Do you know what Father Quinlan says to me this very morning?

SIR PEARCE. Oh, you've seen him already, have you? What did he say?

O'FLAHERTY. He says "You know, don't you," he says, "that it's your duty, as a Christian and a good son of the Holy Church, to love your enemies?" he says. "I know it's my juty as a soldier to kill them," I says. "That's right, Dinny," he says: "quite right. But," says he, "you can kill them and do them a good turn afterward to show your love for them" he says; "and it's your duty to have a mass said for the souls of the hundreds of Germans you say you killed," says he; "for many and many of them were Bavarians and good Catholics," he says. "Is it me that must pay for masses for the souls of the Boshes?" I says. "Let the King of England pay for them," I says; "for it was his quarrel and not mine."

SIR PEARCE [warmly]. It is the quarrel of every honest man and true patriot, O'Flaherty. Your mother must see that as clearly as I do. After all, she is a reasonable, well disposed woman, quite capable of understanding the right and the wrong of the war. Why can't you explain to her what the war is about?

O'FLAHERTY. Arra, sir, how the divil do I know what the war is about?

SIR PEARCE (rising again and standing over him]. What! O'Flaherty: do you know what you are saying? You sit there wearing the Victoria Cross for having killed God knows how many Germans; and you tell me you don't know why you did it!

O'FLAHERTY. Asking your pardon, Sir Pearce, I tell you no such thing. I know quite well why I kilt them, because I was afeard that, if I didn't, they'd kill me.

SIR PEARCE (giving it up, and sitting down again]. Yes, yes, of course; but have you no knowledge of the causes of the war? of the interests at stake? of the importance—I may almost say—in fact I will say—the sacred right for which we are fighting? Don't you read the papers?

O'FLAHERTY. I do when I can get them. There's not many newsboys crying the evening paper in the trenches. They do say, Sir Pearce, that we shall never beat the Boshes until we make Horatio Bottomley Lord Leftnant of England. Do you think that's true, sir?

SIR PEARCE. Rubbish, man! there's no Lord Lieutenant in England: the king is Lord Lieutenant. It's a simple question of patriotism. Does patriotism mean nothing to you?

O'FLAHERTY. It means different to me than what it would to you, sir. It means England and England's king to you. To me and the like of me, it means talking about the English just the way the English papers talk about the Boshes. And what good has it ever done here in Ireland? It's kept me ignorant because it filled up my mother's mind, and she thought it ought to fill up mine too. It's kept Ireland poor, because instead of trying to better ourselves we thought we was the fine fellows of patriots when we were speaking evil of Englishmen that was as poor as ourselves and maybe as good as ourselves. The Boshes I kilt was more knowledgable men than me; and what better am I now that I've kilt them? What better is anybody?

SIR PEARCE [huffed, turning a cold shoulder to him]. I am sorry the terrible experience of this war—the greatest war ever fought —has taught you no better, O'Flaherty.

O'FLAHERTY [preserving his dignity]. I don't know about it's being a great war, sir. It's a big war; but that's not the same thing. Father Quinlan's new church is a big church: you might take the little old chapel out of the middle of it and not miss it. But my mother says there was more true religion in the old chapel. And the war has taught me that maybe she was right.

SIR PEARCE [grunts sulkily]!!

O'FLAHERTY [respectfully but doggedly]. And there's another thing it's taught me too, sir, that concerns you and me, if I may make bold to tell it to you.

SIR PEARCE [still sulky]. I hope it's nothing you oughtn't to say to me, O'Flaherty.

O'FLAHERTY. It's this, sir: that I'm able to sit here now and talk to you without humbugging you; and that's what not one of your tenants or your tenants' childer ever did to you before in all your long life. It's a true respect I'm showing you at last, sir. Maybe you'd rather have me humbug you and tell you lies as I used, just as the boys here, God help them, would rather have me tell them how I fought the Kaiser, that all the world knows I never saw in my life, than tell them the truth. But I can't take advantage of you the way I used, not even if I seem to be wanting in respect to you and cocked up by winning the Cross.

SIR PEARCE [touched]. Not at all, O'Flaherty. Not at all.

O'FLAHERTY. Sure what's the Cross to me, barring the little pension it carries? Do you think I don't know that there's hundreds of men as brave as me that never had the luck to get anything for their bravery but a curse from the sergeant, and the blame for the faults of them that ought to have been their betters? I've learnt more than you'd think, sir; for how would a gentleman like you know what a poor ignorant conceited creature I was when I went from here into the wide world as a soldier? What use is all the lying, and pretending, and humbugging, and letting on, when the day comes to you that your comrade is killed in the trench beside you, and you don't as much as look round at him until you trip over his poor body, and then all you say is to ask why the hell the stretcher–bearers don't take it out of the way. Why should I read the papers to be humbugged and lied to by them that had the cunning to stay at home and send me to fight for them? Don't talk to me or to any soldier of the war being right. No war is right; and all the holy water that Father Quinlan ever blessed couldn't make one right. There, sir! Now you know what O'Flaherty V.C. thinks; and you're wiser so than the others that only knows what he done.

SIR PEARCE [making the best of it, and turning goodhumoredly to him again]. Well, what you did was brave and manly, anyhow.

O'FLAHERTY. God knows whether it was or not, better than you nor me, General. I hope He won't be too hard on me for it, anyhow.

SIR PEARCE [sympathetically]. Oh yes: we all have to think seriously sometimes, especially when we're a little run down. I'm afraid we've been overworking you a bit over these recruiting meetings. However, we can knock off for the rest of the day; and tomorrow's Sunday. I've had about as much as I can stand myself. [He looks at his watch.] It's teatime. I wonder what's keeping your mother.

11

O'Flaherty V.C.

O'FLAHERTY. It's nicely cocked up the old woman will be having tea at the same table as you, sir, instead of in the kitchen. She'll be after dressing in the heighth of grandeur; and stop she will at every house on the way to show herself off and tell them where she's going, and fill the whole parish with spite and envy. But sure, she shouldn't keep you waiting, sir.

SIR PEARCE. Oh, that's all right: she must be indulged on an occasion like this. I'm sorry my wife is in London: she'd have been glad to welcome your mother.

O'FLAHERTY. Sure, I know she would, sir. She was always a kind friend to the poor. Little her ladyship knew, God help her, the depth of divilment that was in us: we were like a play to her. You see, sir, she was English: that was how it was. We was to her what the Pathans and Senegalese was to me when I first seen them: I couldn't think, somehow, that they were liars, and thieves, and backbiters, and drunkards, just like ourselves or any other Christians. Oh, her ladyship never knew all that was going on behind her back: how would she? When I was a weeshy child, she gave me the first penny I ever had in my hand; and I wanted to pray for her conversion that night the same as my mother made me pray for yours; and—

SIR PEARCE [scandalized]. Do you mean to say that your mother made you pray for MY conversion?

O'FLAHERTY. Sure and she wouldn't want to see a gentleman like you going to hell after she nursing your own son and bringing up my sister Annie on the bottle. That was how it was, sir. She'd rob you; and she'd lie to you; and she'd call down all the blessings of God on your head when she was selling you your own three geese that you thought had been ate by the fox the day after you'd finished fattening them, sir; and all the time you were like a bit of her own flesh and blood to her. Often has she said she'd live to see you a good Catholic yet, leading victorious armies against the English and wearing the collar of gold that Malachi won from the proud invader. Oh, she's the romantic woman is my mother, and no mistake.

SIR PEARCE [in great perturbation]. I really can't believe this, O'Flaherty. I could have sworn your mother was as honest a woman as ever breathed.

O'FLAHERTY. And so she is, sir. She's as honest as the day.

12

O'Flaherty V.C.

SIR PEARCE. Do you call it honest to steal my geese?

O'FLAHERTY. She didn't steal them, sir. It was me that stole them.

SIR PEARCE. Oh! And why the devil did you steal them?

O'FLAHERTY. Sure we needed them, sir. Often and often we had to sell our own g
to pay you the rent to satisfy your needs; and why shouldn't we sell your geese to sat
ours?

SIR PEARCE. Well, damn me!

O'FLAHERTY [sweetly]. Sure you had to get what you could out of us; and we had to
get what we could out of you. God forgive us both!

SIR PEARCE. Really, O'Flaherty, the war seems to have upset you a little.

O'FLAHERTY. It's set me thinking, sir; and I'm not used to it. It's like the patriotism of
the English. They never thought of being patriotic until the war broke out; and now the
patriotism has took them so sudden and come so strange to them that they run about like
frightened chickens, uttering all manner of nonsense. But please God they'll forget all
about it when the war's over. They're getting tired of it already.

SIR PEARCE. No, no: it has uplifted us all in a wonderful way. The world will never be
the same again, O'Flaherty. Not after a war like this.

O'FLAHERTY. So they all say, sir. I see no great differ myself. It's all the fright and the
excitement; and when that quiets down they'll go back to their natural divilment and be
the same as ever. It's like the vermin: it'll wash off after a while.

SIR PEARCE [rising and planting himself firmly behind the garden seat]. Well, the long
and the short of it is, O'Flaherty, I must decline to be a party to any attempt to deceive
your mother. I thoroughly disapprove of this feeling against the English, especially at a
moment like the present. Even if your mother's political sympathies are really what you
represent them to be, I should think that her gratitude to Gladstone ought to cure her of
such disloyal prejudices.

O'FLAHERTY [over his shoulder]. She says Gladstone was an Irishman, Sir. What call would he have to meddle with Ireland as he did if he wasn't?

SIR PEARCE. What nonsense! Does she suppose Mr Asquith is an Irishman?

O'FLAHERTY. She won't give him any credit for Home Rule, Sir. She says Redmond made him do it. She says you told her so.

SIR PEARCE [convicted out of his own mouth]. Well, I never meant her to take it up in that ridiculous way. [He moves to the end of the garden seat on O'Flaherty's left.] I'll give her a good talking to when she comes. I'm not going to stand any of her nonsense.

O'FLAHERTY. It's not a bit of use, sir. She says all the English generals is Irish. She says all the English poets and great men was Irish. She says the English never knew how to read their own books until we taught them. She says we're the lost tribes of the house of Israel and the chosen people of God. She says that the goddess Venus, that was born out of the foam of the sea, came up out of the water in Killiney Bay off Bray Head. She says that Moses built the seven churches, and that Lazarus was buried in Glasnevin.

SIR PEARCE. Bosh! How does she know he was? Did you ever ask her?

O'FLAHERTY. I did, sir, often.

SIR PEARCE. And what did she say?

O'FLAHERTY. She asked me how did I know he wasn't, and fetched me a clout on the side of my head.

SIR PEARCE. But have you never mentioned any famous Englishman to her, and asked her what she had to say about him?

O'FLAHERTY. The only one I could think of was Shakespeare, sir; and she says he was born in Cork.

SIR PEARCE [exhausted]. Well, I give it up [he throws himself into the nearest chair]. The woman is—Oh, well! No matter.

O'Flaherty V.C.

O'FLAHERTY [sympathetically]. Yes, sir: she's pigheaded and obstinate: there's no doubt about it. She's like the English: they think there's no one like themselves. It's the same with the Germans, though they're educated and ought to know better. You'll never have a quiet world till you knock the patriotism out of the human race.

SIR PEARCE. Still, we—

O'FLAHERTY. Whisht, sir, for God's sake: here she is.

The General jumps up. Mrs. O'Flaherty arrives and comes between the two men. She is very clean, and carefully dressed in the old fashioned peasant costume; black silk sunbonnet with a tiara of trimmings, and black cloak.

O'FLAHERTY [rising shyly]. Good evening, mother.

MRS O'FLAHERTY [severely]. You hold your whisht, and learn behavior while I pay my juty to his honor. [To Sir Pearce, heartily.] And how is your honor's good self? And how is her ladyship and all the young ladies? Oh, it's right glad we are to see your honor back again and looking the picture of health.

SIR PEARCE [forcing a note of extreme geniality]. Thank you, Mrs O'Flaherty. Well, you see we've brought you back your son safe and sound. I hope you're proud of him.

MRS O'FLAHERTY. And indeed and I am, your honor. It's the brave boy he is; and why wouldn't he be, brought up on your honor's estate and with you before his eyes for a pattern of the finest soldier in Ireland. Come and kiss your old mother, Dinny darlint. [O'Flaherty does so sheepishly.) That's my own darling boy. And look at your fine new uniform stained already with the eggs you've been eating and the porter you've been drinking. [She takes out her handkerchief: spits on it: and scrubs his lapel with it.] Oh, it's the untidy slovenly one you always were. There! It won't be seen on the khaki: it's not like the old red coat that would show up everything that dribbled down on it. [To Sir Pearce.] And they tell me down at the lodge that her ladyship is staying in London, and that Miss Agnes is to be married to a fine young nobleman. Oh, it's your honor that is the lucky and happy father! It will be bad news for many of the young gentlemen of the quality round here, sir. There's lots thought she was going to marry young Master Lawless

15

O'Flaherty V.C.

SIR PEARCE. What! That—that—that bosthoon!

MRS O'FLAHERTY [hilariously]. Let your honor alone for finding the right word! A big bosthoon he is indeed, your honor. Oh, to think of the times and times I have said that Miss Agnes would be my lady as her mother was before her! Didn't I, Dinny?

SIR PEARCE. And now, Mrs. O'Flaherty, I daresay you have a great deal to say to Dennis that doesn't concern me. I'll just go in and order tea.

MRS O'FLAHERTY. Oh, why would your honor disturb yourself? Sure I can take the boy into the yard.

SIR PEARCE. Not at all. It won't disturb me in the least. And he's too big a boy to be taken into the yard now. He has made a front seat for himself. Eh? [He goes into the house.]

MRS O'FLAHERTY. Sure he has that, your honor. God bless your honor! [The General being now out of hearing, she turns threateningly to her son with one of those sudden Irish changes of manner which amaze and scandalize less flexible nations, and exclaims.) And what do you mean, you lying young scald, by telling me you were going to fight agen the English? Did you take me for a fool that couldn't find out, and the papers all full of you shaking hands with the English king at Buckingham Palace?

O'FLAHERTY. I didn't shake hands with him: he shook hands with me. Could I turn on the man in his own house, before his own wife, with his money in my pocket and in yours, and throw his civility back in his face?

MRS O'FLAHERTY. You would take the hand of a tyrant red with the blood of Ireland—

O'FLAHERTY. Arra hold your nonsense, mother: he's not half the tyrant you are, God help him. His hand was cleaner than mine that had the blood of his own relations on it, maybe.

MRS O'FLAHERTY [threateningly]. Is that a way to speak to your mother, you young spalpeen?

16

O'FLAHERTY [stoutly]. It is so, if you won't talk sense to me. It's a nice thing for a poor boy to be made much of by kings and queens, and shook hands with by the heighth of his country's nobility in the capital cities of the world, and then to come home and be scolded and insulted by his own mother. I'll fight for who I like; and I'll shake hands with what kings I like; and if your own son is not good enough for you, you can go and look for another. Do you mind me now?

MRS O'FLAHERTY. And was it the Belgians learned you such brazen impudence?

O'FLAHERTY. The Belgians is good men; and the French ought to be more civil to them, let alone their being half murdered by the Boshes.

MRS O'FLAHERTY. Good men is it! Good men! to come over here when they were wounded because it was a Catholic country, and then to go to the Protestant Church because it didn't cost them anything, and some of them to never go near a church at all. That's what you call good men!

O'FLAHERTY. Oh, you're the mighty fine politician, aren't you? Much you know about Belgians or foreign parts or the world you're living in, God help you!

MRS O'FLAHERTY. Why wouldn't I know better than you? Amment I your mother?

O'FLAHERTY. And if you are itself, how can you know what you never seen as well as me that was dug into the continent of Europe for six months, and was buried in the earth of it three times with the shells bursting on the top of me? I tell you I know what I'm about. I have my own reasons for taking part in this great conflict. I'd be ashamed to stay at home and not fight when everybody else is fighting.

MRS O'FLAHERTY. If you wanted to fight, why couldn't you fight in the German army?

O'FLAHERTY. Because they only get a penny a day.

MRS O'FLAHERTY. Well, and if they do itself, isn't there the French army?

O'FLAHERTY. They only get a hapenny a day.

O'Flaherty V.C.

MRS O'FLAHERTY [much dashed]. Oh murder! They must be a mean lot, Dinny.

O'FLAHERTY [sarcastic]. Maybe you'd have me in the Turkish army, and worship the heathen Mahomet that put a corn in his ear and pretended it was a message from the heavens when the pigeon come to pick it out and eat it. I went where I could get the biggest allowance for you; and little thanks I get for it!

MRS O'FLAHERTY. Allowance, is it! Do you know what the thieving blackguards did on me? They came to me and they says, "Was your son a big eater?" they says. "Oh, he was that," says I: "ten shillings a week wouldn't keep him." Sure I thought the more I said the more they'd give me. "Then," says they, "that's ten shillings a week off your allowance," they says, "because you save that by the king feeding him." "Indeed!" says I: "I suppose if I'd six sons, you'd stop three pound a week from me, and make out that I ought to pay you money instead of you paying me." "There's a fallacy in your argument," they says.

O'FLAHERTY. A what?

MRS O'FLAHERTY. A fallacy: that's the word he said. I says to him, "It's a Pharisee I'm thinking you mean, sir; but you can keep your dirty money that your king grudges a poor old widow; and please God the English will be bet yet for the deadly sin of oppressing the poor"; and with that I shut the door in his face.

O'FLAHERTY [furious]. Do you tell me they knocked ten shillings off you for my keep?

MRS O'FLAHERTY [soothing him]. No, darlint: they only knocked off half a crown. I put up with it because I've got the old age pension; and they know very well I'm only sixty–two; so I've the better of them by half a crown a week anyhow.

O'FLAHERTY. It's a queer way of doing business. If they'd tell you straight out what they was going to give you, you wouldn't mind; but if there was twenty ways of telling the truth and only one way of telling a lie, the Government would find it out. It's in the nature of governments to tell lies.

Teresa Driscoll, a parlor maid, comes from the house,

18

O'Flaherty V.C.

TERESA. You're to come up to the drawing–room to have your tea, Mrs. O'Flaherty.

MRS O'FLAHERTY. Mind you have a sup of good black tea for me in the kitchen afterwards, acushla. That washy drawing–room tea will give me the wind if I leave it on my stomach. [She goes into the house, leaving the two young people alone together.]

O'FLAHERTY. Is that yourself, Tessie? And how are you?

TERESA. Nicely, thank you. And how's yourself?

O'FLAHERTY. Finely, thank God. [He produces a gold chain.] Look what I've brought you, Tessie.

TERESA [shrinking]. Sure I don't like to touch it, Denny. Did you take it off a dead man?

O'FLAHERTY. No: I took it off a live one; and thankful he was to me to be alive and kept a prisoner in ease and comfort, and me left fighting in peril of my life.

TERESA [taking it]. Do you think it's real gold, Denny?

O'FLAHERTY. It's real German gold, anyhow.

TERESA. But German silver isn't real, Denny.

O'FLAHERTY [his face darkening]. Well, it's the best the Bosh could do for me, anyhow.

TERESA. Do you think I might take it to the jeweller next market day and ask him?

O'FLAHERTY [sulkily]. You may take it to the divil if you like.

TERESA. You needn't lose your temper about it. I only thought I'd like to know. The nice fool I'd look if I went about showing off a chain that turned out to be only brass!

O'FLAHERTY. I think you might say Thank you.

TERESA. Do you? I think you might have said something more to me than "Is that yourself?" You couldn't say less to the postman.

O'FLAHERTY [his brow clearing]. Oh, is that what's the matter? Here! come and take the taste of ther brass out of my mouth. [He seizes her and kisses her.]

Teresa, without losing her Irish dignity, takes the kiss as appreciatively as a connoisseur might take a glass of wine, and sits down with him on the garden seat,

TERESA [as he squeezes her waist]. Thank God the priest can't see us here!

O'FLAHERTY. It's little they care for priests in France, alanna.

TERESA. And what had the queen on her, Denny, when she spoke to you in the palace?

O'FLAHERTY. She had a bonnet on without any strings to it. And she had a plakeen of embroidery down her bosom. And she had her waist where it used to be, and not where the other ladies had it. And she had little brooches in her ears, though she hadn't half the jewelry of Mrs Sullivan that keeps the popshop in Drumpogue. And she dresses her hair down over her forehead, in a fringe like. And she has an Irish look about her eyebrows. And she didn't know what to say to me, poor woman! and I didn't know what to say to her, God help me!

TERESA. You'll have a pension now with the Cross, won't you, Denny?

O'FLAHERTY. Sixpence three farthings a day.

TERESA. That isn't much.

O'FLAHERTY. I take out the rest in glory.

TERESA. And if you're wounded, you'll have a wound pension, won't you?

O'FLAHERTY. I will, please God.

TERESA. You're going out again, aren't you, Denny?

O'FLAHERTY. I can't help myself. I'd be shot for a deserter if I didn't go; and maybe I'll be shot by the Boshes if I do go; so between the two of them I'm nicely fixed up.

MRS O'FLAHERTY [calling from within the house]. Tessie! Tessie darlint!

TERESA [disengaging herself from his arm and rising]. I'm wanted for the tea table. You'll have a pension anyhow, Denny, won't you, whether you're wounded or not?

MRS O'FLAHERTY. Come, child, come.

TERESA [impatiently]. Oh, sure I'm coming. [She tries to smile at Denny, not very convincingly, and hurries into the house.]

O'FLAHERTY [alone]. And if I do get a pension itself, the divil a penny of it you'll ever have the spending of.

MRS O'FLAHERTY [as she comes from the porch]. Oh, it's a shame for you to keep the girl from her juties, Dinny. You might get her into trouble.

O'FLAHERTY. Much I care whether she gets into trouble or not! I pity the man that gets her into trouble. He'll get himself into worse.

MRS O'FLAHERTY. What's that you tell me? Have you been falling out with her, and she a girl with a fortune of ten pounds?

O'FLAHERTY. Let her keep her fortune. I wouldn't touch her with the tongs if she had thousands and millions.

MRS O'FLAHERTY. Oh fie for shame, Dinny! why would you say the like of that of a decent honest girl, and one of the Driscolls too?

O'FLAHERTY. Why wouldn't I say it? She's thinking of nothing but to get me out there again to be wounded so that she may spend my pension, bad scran to her!

MRS O'FLAHERTY. Why, what's come over you, child, at all at all?

21

O'Flaherty V.C.

O'FLAHERTY. Knowledge and wisdom has come over me with pain and fear and trouble. I've been made a fool of and imposed upon all my life. I thought that covetious sthreal in there was a walking angel; and now if ever I marry at all I'll marry a Frenchwoman.

MRS O'FLARERTY [fiercely]. You'll not, so; and don't you dar repeat such a thing to me.

O'FLAHERTY. Won't I, faith! I've been as good as married to a couple of them already.

MRS O'FLAHERTY. The Lord be praised, what wickedness have you been up to, you young blackguard?

O'FLAHERTY. One of them Frenchwomen would cook you a meal twice in the day and all days and every day that Sir Pearce himself might go begging through Ireland for, and never see the like of. I'll have a French wife, I tell you; and when I settle down to be a farmer I'll have a French farm, with a field as big as the continent of Europe that ten of your dirty little fields here wouldn't so much as fill the ditch of.

MRS O'FLAHERTY [furious]. Then it's a French mother you may go look for; for I'm done with you.

O'FLAHERTY. And it's no great loss you'd be if it wasn't for my natural feelings for you; for it's only a silly ignorant old countrywoman you are with all your fine talk about Ireland: you that never stepped beyond the few acres of it you were born on!

MRS O'FLAHERTY [tottering to the garden seat and showing signs of breaking down]. Dinny darlint, why are you like this to me? What's happened to you?

O'FLAHERTY [gloomily]. What's happened to everybody? that's what I want to know. What's happened to you that I thought all the world of and was afeard of? What's happened to Sir Pearce, that I thought was a great general, and that I now see to be no more fit to command an army than an old hen? What's happened to Tessie, that I was mad to marry a year ago, and that I wouldn't take now with all Ireland for her fortune? I tell you the world's creation is crumbling in ruins about me; and then you come and ask what's happened to me?

O'Flaherty V.C.

MRS O'FLAHERTY [giving way to wild grief]. Ochone! ochone! my son's turned agen me. Oh, what'll I do at all at all? Oh! oh! oh! oh!

SIR PEARCE [running out of the house]. What's this infernal noise? What on earth is the matter?

O'FLAHERTY. Arra hold your whisht, mother. Don't you see his honor?

MRS O'FLAHERTY. Oh, Sir, I'm ruined and destroyed. Oh, won't you speak to Dinny, Sir: I'm heart scalded with him. He wants to marry a Frenchwoman on me, and to go away and be a foreigner and desert his mother and betray his country. It's mad he is with the roaring of the cannons and he killing the Germans and the Germans killing him, bad cess to them! My boy is taken from me and turned agen me; and who is to take care of me in my old age after all I've done for him, ochone! ochone!

O'FLAHERTY. Hold your noise, I tell you. Who's going to leave you? I'm going to take you with me. There now: does that satisfy you?

MRS O'FLAHERTY. Is it take me into a strange land among heathens and pagans and savages, and me not knowing a word of their language nor them of mine?

O'FLAHERTY. A good job they don't: maybe they'll think you're talking sense.

MRS O'FLAHERTY. Ask me to die out of Ireland, is it? and the angels not to find me when they come for me!

O'FLAHERTY. And would you ask me to live in Ireland where I've been imposed on and kept in ignorance, and to die where the divil himself wouldn't take me as a gift, let alone the blessed angels? You can come or stay. You can take your old way or take my young way. But stick in this place I will not among a lot of good−for−nothing divils that'll not do a hand's turn but watch the grass growing and build up the stone wall where the cow walked through it. And Sir Horace Plunkett breaking his heart all the time telling them how they might put the land into decent tillage like the French and Belgians.

SIR PEARCE. Yes, he's quite right, you know, Mrs O'Flaherty: quite right there.

O'Flaherty V.C.

MRS O'FLAHERTY. Well, sir, please God the war will last a long time yet; and maybe I'll die before it's over and the separation allowance stops.

O'FLAHERTY. That's all you care about. It's nothing but milch cows we men are for the women, with their separation allowances, ever since the war began, bad luck to them that made it!

TERESA [coming from the porch between the General and Mrs O'Flaherty. Hannah sent me out for to tell you, sir, that the tea will be black and the cake not fit to eat with the cold if yous all don't come at wanst.

MRS O'FLAHERTY [breaking out again]. Oh, Tessie darlint, what have you been saying to Dinny at all at all? Oh! Oh—

SIR PEARCE [out of patience]. You can't discuss that here. We shall have Tessie beginning now.

O'FLAHERTY. That's right, sir: drive them in.

TERESA. I haven't said a word to him. He—

SIR PEARCE. Hold your tongue; and go in and attend to your business at the tea table.

TERESA. But amment I telling your honor that I never said a word to him? He gave me a beautiful gold chain. Here it is to show your honor that it's no lie I'm telling you.

SIR PEARCE. What's this, O'Flaherty? You've been looting some unfortunate officer.

O'FLAHERTY. No, sir: I stole it from him of his own accord.

MRS O'FLAHERTY. Wouldn't your honor tell him that his mother has the first call on it? What would a slip of a girl like that be doing with a gold chain round her neck?

TERESA [venomously]. Anyhow, I have a neck to put it round and not a hank of wrinkles.

24

O'Flaherty V.C.

At this unfortunate remark, Mrs O'Flaherty bounds from her seat: and an appalling tempest of wordy wrath breaks out. The remonstrances and commands of the General, and the protests and menaces of O'Flaherty, only increase the hubbub. They are soon all speaking at once at the top of their voices.

MRS O'FLAHERTY [solo]. You impudent young heifer, how dar you say such a thing to me? [Teresa retorts furiously: the men interfere: and the solo becomes a quartet, fortissimo.] I've a good mind to clout your ears for you to teach you manners. Be ashamed of yourself, do; and learn to know who you're speaking to. That I maytn't sin! but I don't know what the good God was thinking about when he made the like of you. Let me not see you casting sheep's eyes at my son again. There never was an O'Flaherty yet that would demean himself by keeping company with a dirty Driscoll; and if I see you next or nigh my house I'll put you in the ditch with a flea in your ear: mind that now.

TERESA. Is it me you offer such a name to, you fou–mouthed, dirty–minded, lying, sloothering old sow, you? I wouldn't soil my tongue by calling you in your right name and telling Sir Pearce what's the common talk of the town about you. You and your O'Flahertys! setting yourself up agen the Driscolls that would never lower themselves to be seen in conversation with you at the fair. You can keep your ugly stingy lump of a son; for what is he but a common soldier? and God help the girl that gets him, say I! So the back of my hand to you, Mrs O'Flaherty; and that the cat may tear your ugly old face!

SIR PEARCE. Silence. Tessie, did you hear me ordering you to go into the house? Mrs O'Flaherty! [Louder.] Mrs O'Flaherty!! Will you just listen to me one moment? Please. [Furiously.] Do you hear me speaking to you, woman? Are you human beings or are you wild beasts? Stop that noise immediately: do you hear? [Yelling.] Are you going to do what I order you, or are you not? Scandalous! Disgraceful! This comes of being too familiar with you. O'Flaherty, shove them into the house. Out with the whole damned pack of you.

O'FLAHERTY [to the women]. Here now: none of that, none of that. Go easy, I tell you. Hold your whisht, mother, will you, or you'll be sorry for it after. [To Teresa.] Is that the way for a decent young girl to speak? [Despairingly.] Oh, for the Lord's sake, shut up, will yous? Have you no respect for yourselves or your betters? [Peremptorily.] Let me have no more of it, I tell you. Och! the divil's in the whole crew of you. In with you into the house this very minute and tear one another's eyes out in the kitchen if you like. In with you.

The two men seize the two women, and push them, still violently abusing one another, into the house. Sir Pearce slams the door upon them savagely. Immediately a heavenly silence falls on the summer afternoon. The two sit down out of breath: and for a long time nothing is said. Sir Pearce sits on an iron chair. O'Flaherty sits on the garden seat. The thrush begins to sing melodiously. O'Flaherty cocks his ears, and looks up at it. A smile spreads over his troubled features. Sir Pearce, with a long sigh, takes out his pipe and begins to fill it.

O'FLAHERTY [idyllically]. What a discontented sort of an animal a man is, sir! Only a month ago, I was in the quiet of the country out at the front, with not a sound except the birds and the bellow of a cow in the distance as it might be, and the shrapnel making little clouds in the heavens, and the shells whistling, and maybe a yell or two when one of us was hit; and would you believe it, sir, I complained of the noise and wanted to have a peaceful hour at home. Well: them two has taught me a lesson. This morning, sir, when I was telling the boys here how I was longing to be back taking my part for king and country with the others, I was lying, as you well knew, sir. Now I can go and say it with a clear conscience. Some likes war's alarums; and some likes home life. I've tried both, sir; and I'm for war's alarums now. I always was a quiet lad by natural disposition.

SIR PEARCE. Strictly between ourselves, O'Flaherty, and as one soldier to another [O'Flaherty salutes, but without stiffening], do you think we should have got an army without conscription if domestic life had been as happy as people say it is?

O'FLAHERTY. Well, between you and me and the wall, Sir Pearce, I think the less we say about that until the war's over, the better.

He winks at the General. The General strikes a match. The thrush sings. A jay laughs. The conversation drops.

Printed in the United Kingdom
by Lightning Source UK Ltd.
126407UK00001BA/21/A